# Quiet Times
## FOR
# Busy Moms

**52 Devotions**

**BroadStreet**
PUBLISHING

BroadStreet Publishing Group, LLC
Racine, Wisconsin, USA
BroadStreetPublishing.com

Quiet Times for Busy Moms: 52 Devotions

Written by Vicki Kuyper

Copyright © 2017 by BroadStreet Publishing Group

ISBN-13: 978-1-4245-5414-0 (hardcover)
ISBN-13: 978-1-4245-5415-7 (e-book)

Stock or custom editions of BroadStreet Publishing titles may be purchased in bulk for educational, business, ministry, fundraising, or sales promotional use. For information, please e-mail info@broadstreetpublishing.com.

Cover design by Chris Garborg at garborgdesign.com
Interior design and typeset by Katherine Lloyd theDESKonline.com

Printed in China

17 18 19 20 21 5 4 3 2 1

# Contents

1 The Marathon of Motherhood .................................... 5

2 The Ultimate Do-Over ........................................... 8

3 Mother of Thunder ............................................. 11

4 The Power of Friendship ........................................ 14

5 I'm Bored! ..................................................... 17

6 Close at Heart ................................................. 20

7 Clearing the Clutter ........................................... 23

8 Kids at Heart .................................................. 26

9 Queen Mom .................................................... 29

10 Words of Life ................................................. 32

11 Quiet, Please! ................................................ 35

12 Room to Grow ................................................ 38

13 Making the Miles Count ...................................... 41

14 A Cry for Help ............................................... 44

15 Dressed to Bless ............................................. 47

16 Belief or Make-Believe? ..................................... 50

17 Taken by Surprise ............................................ 53

18 The Blessing of Buffering .................................... 56

19 Beyond Compare ............................................. 59

20 What's Really Mine? ......................................... 62

21 Put Yourself in Time-Out! .................................... 65

22 All Together Now ............................................ 68

23 Chew on This ................................................ 71

24 We Are Family ............................................... 74

25 Prime Time .................................................. 77

26  Mental Gymnastics . . . . . . . . . . . . . . . . . . . . . . . . . . . . . . . . . 80

27  Sibling Rivalry . . . . . . . . . . . . . . . . . . . . . . . . . . . . . . . . . . . . 83

28  Rash Guard . . . . . . . . . . . . . . . . . . . . . . . . . . . . . . . . . . . . . . 86

29  Jesus: Problem Child? . . . . . . . . . . . . . . . . . . . . . . . . . . . . . . 89

30  Focus on the Positive . . . . . . . . . . . . . . . . . . . . . . . . . . . . . . 92

31  Rebel or Reformer? . . . . . . . . . . . . . . . . . . . . . . . . . . . . . . . . 95

32  A Bounty of Blessing . . . . . . . . . . . . . . . . . . . . . . . . . . . . . . . 98

33  No Excuses . . . . . . . . . . . . . . . . . . . . . . . . . . . . . . . . . . . . . . 101

34  Everything in Its Place . . . . . . . . . . . . . . . . . . . . . . . . . . . . . 104

35  Mother's Little Helper . . . . . . . . . . . . . . . . . . . . . . . . . . . . . 107

36  A True Gem . . . . . . . . . . . . . . . . . . . . . . . . . . . . . . . . . . . . . . 110

37  Carpe Diem Goes Digital . . . . . . . . . . . . . . . . . . . . . . . . . . . . 113

38  Peacemaker Mom . . . . . . . . . . . . . . . . . . . . . . . . . . . . . . . . . 116

39  Messy Me . . . . . . . . . . . . . . . . . . . . . . . . . . . . . . . . . . . . . . . 119

40  One Step at a Time . . . . . . . . . . . . . . . . . . . . . . . . . . . . . . . . 122

41  Undercover Mother . . . . . . . . . . . . . . . . . . . . . . . . . . . . . . . . 125

42  We All Need a Hero . . . . . . . . . . . . . . . . . . . . . . . . . . . . . . . . 128

43  Refresh and Renew . . . . . . . . . . . . . . . . . . . . . . . . . . . . . . . . 131

44  Love Conquers All . . . . . . . . . . . . . . . . . . . . . . . . . . . . . . . . . 134

45  One of a Kind . . . . . . . . . . . . . . . . . . . . . . . . . . . . . . . . . . . . 137

46  Family Fanfare . . . . . . . . . . . . . . . . . . . . . . . . . . . . . . . . . . . 140

47  Walk This Way . . . . . . . . . . . . . . . . . . . . . . . . . . . . . . . . . . . 143

48  Repeat Performance . . . . . . . . . . . . . . . . . . . . . . . . . . . . . . . 146

49  Time to Lend a Hand . . . . . . . . . . . . . . . . . . . . . . . . . . . . . . 149

50  All in Good Time . . . . . . . . . . . . . . . . . . . . . . . . . . . . . . . . . . 152

51  Feel Free to Get the Giggles . . . . . . . . . . . . . . . . . . . . . . . . . 155

52  Our Bittersweet Blessing . . . . . . . . . . . . . . . . . . . . . . . . . . . . 158

# The Marathon of Motherhood

Therefore, since we are surrounded by such a
great cloud of witnesses, let us throw off everything
that hinders and the sin that so easily entangles.
And let us run with perseverance the race
marked out for us, fixing our eyes on Jesus,
the pioneer and perfecter of faith.

—HEBREWS 12:1–2

Being a mom is one of God's greatest gifts. But, it can also be one of life's greatest challenges. It's like running a marathon wearing a baby carrier. It takes plenty of hard work just to get to the starting line. Then, once the actual race begins, it feels like it goes on forever. Sure, you may enjoy running the first ten, fifteen, or even twenty miles, but then you hit a wall, and it takes all of the faith, courage, and perseverance you can muster just to keep putting one foot in front of the other.

But, we don't run alone. Scripture tells us there's a "great cloud of witnesses" (Hebrews 12:1) that surround us, cheering us on with their encouragement and example. Take Susanna Wesley. She was the mother of Charles Wesley, who wrote over six thousand hymns, and John Wesley, who became a great evangelist. She gave birth to nineteen children, only ten of whom lived beyond infancy. Her husband was a preacher who was by all accounts an incredibly difficult man. Their home burned down twice, presumably by church members who didn't agree with what her husband said from the pulpit. They were deep in debt. And, she was often ill. Yet, Susanna found a way to persevere. Even today, over 250 years after her death, she remains a mom worth emulating.

When she needed time out, Susanna would throw her apron over her head and pray. Her kids knew this simple act meant, *Do not disturb!* Like Susanna, each of us needs a proverbial apron where we can take a break from the demands of motherhood and find the strength to continue the race God's set before us. Connecting with God in prayer throughout the day can help us find a place of peace—and power—amidst the chaos.

Dear Lord, life gets so hectic that some days I forget you are near. Help me develop a habit of prayer and a longing to connect with you throughout the day, especially the busy ones. Amen.

A TIP TO TRY: Choose your own personal "prayer apron." It could be a "time-out" chair, the bathtub (preferably for a bubble bath), or even a literal apron (whether you wear it over your head or not is up to you). What's important is that your kids recognize it as a signal that Mom needs time out to pray.

2

# The Ultimate Do-Over

Make allowance for each other's faults,
and forgive anyone who offends you.
Remember, the Lord forgave you,
so you must forgive others.

—COLOSSIANS 3:13 NLT

We all wish we had perfect children; kids who never spilled their milk, played in the toilet, or talked back. But let's face it: it's genetic. No kid has a perfect mom, so why should we expect from our children what we ourselves cannot accomplish as grown-ups? All of us, big and little, need forgiveness and a fresh start. Every day. Graciously, God provides us with exactly what we need.

God's unique solution to our ongoing problem is for his Son's perfect life to cover our imperfect one. Through

Jesus' sacrificial death on the cross, he erased every wrong choice we would make throughout our lives. However, it doesn't mean our misdeeds don't matter. In fact, they matter so much they cost Jesus his life. The weight of this truth is a heavy one to bear, but God doesn't want us to live weighed down by guilt and shame, working hard to fulfill a debt we can never repay. His forgiveness comes wrapped in the free gift of grace. To receive it, all we need to do is ask.

The Bible describes this as being "born again" (John 3:1–21)—the ultimate do-over. Talk about a fresh start! But understanding and accepting God's forgiveness is only the beginning. Next comes forgiving others, as well as ourselves. Letting go of mistakes, selfish choices, harsh words, betrayal, or emotional wounds (especially ones where the consequences continue on long after the initial offense has passed) is far from easy, but past offenses belong to yesterday. Today is a brand-new day for us and for those we love. Let's allow God to help us live it to the fullest!

Dear Lord, thank you for all you've forgiven me—from my silliest mistakes to my most selfish and rebellious words and deeds. Show me how to extend that same grace and forgiveness to those around me, including my children. Amen.

A TIP TO TRY: Because of God's inexhaustible forgiveness, we can pray, "Wash me, and I will be whiter than snow" (Psalm 51:7). However, when it comes to cleaning crayon off a white wall, use baby oil on a clean white rag or try a baby wipe.

# Mother of Thunder

"What do you want?" Jesus asked her. She answered,
"Promise me that these two sons of mine will sit at
your right and your left when you are King."

—MATTHEW 20:21 GNB

Our kids are exceptional. We knew it from the moment they were born. Of course, we're not the only mom who sees their kids this way. For example, take the mother of James and John, two of Jesus' disciples (nicknamed, by Jesus, the Sons of Thunder), who was equally capable of stirring up quite a storm. Even though Jesus chose twelve young men to follow him, this mom (and her sons) felt no hesitation in asking that they be pushed to the head of the line to be eternally honored in an exceptional way.

Yes, good mothers love their kids deeply. And when

we love someone, we want the best for them. However, just because the depth of our love raises our children to the level of "exceptional" in our eyes, it doesn't mean they're entitled to become an exception to the rules.

So when our children don't win first place, are overlooked for the soccer team, or turn in a homework assignment late and suffer the consequences of a lower grade, let's not leap to their defense. Instead, let's show them how to celebrate someone else's victory, to find joy in serving others, and to handle disappointment and failure with grace, rather than always having to be king of the hill.

Jesus' response to the request by the Mother of Thunder (and to the resulting offense taken by the rest of the disciples) was, "If one of you wants to be great, you must be the servant of the rest" (Matthew 20:26 GNB). What makes people truly exceptional is when they don't have to be the center of attention or have everything their way. Instead, they find contentment and purpose in loving others well and serving outside the spotlight. Sounds a bit like motherhood, don't you think?

Dear Lord, please show me how to be my children's advocate without pushing them ahead of everyone else. When it comes to my family, help me hold tightly to truth and humility, as well as love. Amen.

A TIP TO TRY: Help your kids' view of the world extend beyond their own lives. Make a bedtime Prayer Chain. Have each child write prayer requests for friends and family on strips of construction paper. Link them together into a chain. Use it as a touchstone for prayer every evening. Add links for new requests and remove links when prayers are answered—use them to create an Answered Prayer Chain.

# The Power of Friendship

Sweet friendships refresh the soul and awaken
our hearts with joy, for good friends
are like the anointing oil that yields the
fragrant incense of God's presence.

—Proverbs 27:9 TPT

It's amazing how we can be surrounded by children all day and still feel so alone. Even though motherhood isn't a solitary job, it can be an isolating one, particularly if we don't work outside the home. But, it doesn't have to be. Staying connected with friends can be a lifeline during crazy times.

Consider King David and his Mighty Warriors (2 Samuel 23:8–39). Though David's responsibilities were different than yours are today, being king was stressful and challenging in its own way, as well as potentially isolating. So, David surrounded himself with thirty men of valor and courage, three of whom he considered his right-hand men. They fought for him and with him. Regardless of the circumstances, David knew these men were always on his side.

Who are the Mighty Women in your life? Who'll fight for you and with you to help you become the woman God created you to be? Who consistently provides wise advice, a godly perspective, and words of encouragement? These are relationships worth nurturing throughout your lifetime.

Though your free time is limited right now, do what you can to stay connected: Text a picture of your crazy day, if you don't have time to call. Gather a small group of moms and their kids for a play date. Trade babysitting time with one another. And make time for some girl time, even if it's just one evening out a month.

If you don't already have a group of friends that fit the bill, rustle up the courage to reach out. Start a mom's group at church or invite other moms in your neighborhood to an informal get-together. You may be the Mighty Woman another woman is praying to connect with right now.

Dear Lord, thank you for the friends you've brought into my life. Please show me how to be a faithful friend, even when my time is limited. Teach me how to love and listen well. Amen.

A TIP TO TRY: If you have trouble finding time to connect with friends in person, especially those who don't live nearby, send a one-minute video blog via text message each week. Rehearse before you record, trying to squeeze the highlights and struggles of the past week all into 60 seconds. Then, ask your friends to do the same for you. (Warning: this may become a highlight of your week!)

# I'm Bored!

Above all else, guard your heart,
for everything you do flows from it.

—PROVERBS 4:23

We're not born bored. Even though a baby's "world" has a relatively limited scope, exploration is the name of the game. For an infant, discovering a piece of fuzz on the carpet or mastering the dexterity it takes to hold a toy is akin to Columbus discovering America. A year later, a simple cardboard box can become a ship, a castle, a plane, or a toddler's version of CrossFit, as they climb in and out over and over again.

Over time, however, children develop a "been there, played with that" mentality, which is often carried straight into adulthood. Chances are we can attest to this firsthand. That longing for what's new, improved, bigger, or better strikes us most strongly when we're bored. Bored with what we own. Bored with what we're doing. Sometimes, even bored with whom we've chosen to marry.

But, the root of boredom isn't circumstantial; it's spiritual. It's discontent in disguise. When we say "I'm bored," we're telling God that what he's provided isn't enough, which means it's a change of heart, not situation, that's needed most. This is true for us, as well as our children.

When it comes to our children, God made us mothers not cruise directors. When our kids say, "I'm bored," it isn't our job to keep them happily entertained every minute of the day. We do, however, need to discern whether their boredom stems from discontent, feeling neglected (because we're not paying enough attention to them), tired, overstimulated, or frustrated with what they're currently doing. If their boredom stems from discontent, it's best to allow them to get bored with being bored. Give their imagination time to kick in. Allow them the chance to rediscover the blessing of what they already own. This skill will serve them well into adulthood.

Dear Lord, I know I'm as guilty as my kids for always wanting more. Give me fresh eyes to clearly see how generously you've provided for us. Amen.

A TIP TO TRY: Help your children learn how to play independently by creating a Boredom Box. Fill it with slips of paper, each listing one simple chore that needs to be done around the house. Anytime your kids say, "I'm bored," they draw a slip from the box that will give them something to do. Chances are they'll try to be more creative in filling their own time, instead of drawing from the box.

# 6

# Close at Heart

He tends his flock like a shepherd:
He gathers the lambs in his arms and
carries them close to his heart;
he gently leads those that have young.

—ISAIAH 40:11

How handy it would be if every newborn came with an instruction booklet. If we only knew exactly what to do to ensure that our children would grow up to be happy, healthy, godly adults, we'd strive to follow every guideline to a tee. However, motherhood is much more subjective than that. Every day is filled with choices that are nowhere close to black and white.

Take diapers. We have an entire grocery store aisle of brands from which to sort through and choose. This doesn't even take into account the option of using cloth diapers, or a diaper service, or which diaper rash cream to purchase, or how frequently we should use it.

There's also plenty of advice to go around, courtesy of our pediatrician, reference books, online resources, support groups, other moms, relatives, complete strangers, and our own sleep-deprived intuition. But there comes a time when we need to stop weighing our options and decide. We can't research diapers forever. Once the baby arrives we have to slap one on and call it good.

With so many decisions to make about our children's physical, emotional, educational, relational, and spiritual needs, all we really can do is weigh and pray. We can pray for the Holy Spirit's guidance each and every day. We can weigh the knowledge and advice we receive against God's guidance and our own good sense. Then, we need to make a decision and follow through.

We can't possibly know it all, but we can trust the One who does. He's always near, loving us, guiding us, and holding us and our family close to his heart.

Dear Lord, I've never needed your wisdom more in my life. Help me be the mother my children need—one who honors you in all that I do. Amen.

A TIP TO TRY: There are lots of great parenting ideas we can glean from magazines, blogs, and tips from friends and family, but when life gets busy, it's easy to forget what we're sure we'll remember. Keep a box of 3 x 5 cards divided into sections such as: activities, discipline, meal times, and health. Anytime you hear or read a tip you'd like to try, write it on a card and file it for later use. Writing it down will help you recall it more easily.

# 7

# Clearing the Clutter

We didn't bring anything into this world,
and we won't take anything with us when we leave.

—1 TIMOTHY 6:7 CEV

How much of a mother's day revolves around cleaning, organizing, maintaining, mending, buying, or getting rid of stuff? A considerable amount. It's true that some of the stuff is incredibly useful, some of it is sentimentally significant, and yes, some of it is just plain fun, but everything we own comes with a commitment. We have to figure out how to use it, find a place to keep it, and take care of it. If we don't, we're wasting the resources God has given us.

However, the stuff we own does more than simply take up space in our home and time in our day; it also has a hold on our heart. Sometimes we tie what we own to our own self-worth. Whether it's the label on our jeans, the size of our home, or the make of our car, we sometimes use possessions to let others know we're successful, and therefore, important. And if our desire to acquire fuels us to live beyond our means, our possessions are no longer just stuff; they become idols we worship, masters we serve, and false gods we believe can fulfill us and make us happy.

It's easy to fall into a trapdoor of materialism and drag our kids right down with us. When we try to make them happy by giving them more "stuff," we're setting them up for discontentment. The truth is, what we hold in our hands can never adequately fill our hearts. Only God's presence can do that. The closer we draw to God, the less stuff we realize we "need" to be content. Love, joy, peace, and deep-hearted relationships with others are the things that fill our heart to the brim—without adding any clutter to our home.

Dear Lord, I know I get attached to stuff. I desire things I don't need, but I still long to own them. I want my contentment to be rooted solely in you. Only you can show me how. Amen.

A TIP TO TRY: To help kids learn to hold more loosely to possessions, challenge them to donate something they already own every time they get something new. Are you willing to do the same?

# 8 Kids at Heart

It's wonderful to be young!
Enjoy every minute of it!
—Ecclesiastes 11:9 NLT

Having kids can make you feel old, even while you're still young! Sleep deprivation, the repetitiveness of household chores, disciplinary skirmishes, and winding up in the deep end of a car pool can leave you exhausted—and dreaming of the day you can sit on the porch of an old folks' home in a rocker. But let's not grow old before our time. Despite the daily challenges of parenting, our kids are experts at teaching us how to stay young at heart. We simply need to learn to be more attentive students.

On the days when our kids are pushing us to the limit—mentally, physically, and spiritually—let's stop, take a breath, and reflect instead of automatically heading into response mode. Their misdeeds may be rooted more in youth and immaturity than disobedience and rebellion. Why are they making the choices they are right now? Are they confused, frustrated, or tired? What were we like at their age? How did we learn the lessons we long for them to learn? Or did we? Are we still exhibiting the same behavior they are, only in a more "grown-up" fashion?

And on those glorious days when our kids let their imaginations call the shots; when they're having so much fun they lose all concept of time; and when they can't stop giggling or are rendered speechless by some wonder of God's creation, let's allow their innocence, curiosity, and awe to turn back the hands of time for us. They have much to teach us about abandoning ourselves to lifelong joy.

God has given us to each other—mother and child— one leading and one learning, but who's to say which is which at any given moment? Whether in joy or in challenge, what do our children have to teach us today?

Dear Lord, let my children bring out the child in me. Let me remember what it's like to walk in shoes as small as theirs. Help me to be open and attentive enough to learn from them today. Amen.

A TIP TO TRY: Switch roles this weekend and let your kids plan a family day together. Give them a budget and a time frame. Then do all you can to make their ideas become reality. Their creativity and unique view of fun may open your family up to a few new paths of adventure.

# Queen Mom

9

"Who knows if perhaps you were
made queen for just such a time as this?"
—ESTHER 4:14 NLT

Many of us are familiar with the Old Testament story
of Esther—the beautiful Jewish orphan who wound
up as queen of Susa, the capital of Persia. She risked her
life by asking for an audience with the rather fickle king,
where she revealed her Jewish heritage and pleaded for
the life of her fellow Jews. By risking her own life, she
saved it, as well as the lives of God's people.

As queen, Esther was in a unique position of influence
and power—a position that assured her choices would
have a widespread impact on the lives of others. Believe
it or not, you and Esther have a lot in common in this
area. You may not feel like a queen, but you are co-ruler

of the kingdom of your household. You are in a powerful position, one that will have an effect on your children for the rest of their lives.

Think back to your own childhood. Which words, actions, and decisions your parents made were turning points in your own life? How did they influence who you grew up to be? We never know when what we say or do will become a watershed moment for our own children, for better or for worse.

Let's not take our power lightly. What we say offhandedly may be something our child takes to heart for years to come. One decision we make may influence our children's future choice of career or spouse, whether they pursue or bury a talent God's given them, and how they see themselves in the eyes of God and others. Yes, God's power in their lives can certainly cover any of our mistakes, but let's be aware of the power we hold and use it in a gracious, godly way.

Dear Lord, it's so easy to fall into a rut of motherhood, where every new day feels a lot like the one that's just passed. Open my eyes and heart to the significance of every interaction I have with my kids. Help me love them well. Amen.

A TIP TO TRY: If you have young girls who like to play princess, there's bound to be unwanted glitter around your home. Clean it up easily with a ball of play dough. The addition of glitter will make the play dough even more fun for future use!

# Words of Life

When you speak healing words, you offer others
fruit from the tree of life. But unhealthy, negative
words do nothing but crush their hopes.

—PROVERBS 15:4 TPT

We do what we can to keep our kids healthy, including feeding them a balanced diet. We know their
bodies will function differently if we serve them a meal
high in protein with a side of veggies, as opposed to a buffet of jelly beans, french fries, donut holes, and soda, but
when we're running short on time and energy, fast food is
cheaper, more expedient, and also tastes pretty good on
the way down. However, just because something's quick
and easy doesn't mean it's best.

Take our words, for instance. When we're out in public, we're usually more thoughtful about what we allow out of our mouths. We choose to offer more balanced opinions and emotions. At home is where we let our true colors shine. This can mean that those we love most receive the worst we have to offer. Some of the things we allow to slip past our lips are not merely junk food; they're like feeding our family poison.

Words go into our minds and hearts just like food goes into our bodies. They can nourish, help, and heal or wound, scar, and destroy. The choice is ours. James 1:19 reminds us, "Everyone should be quick to listen, slow to speak and slow to become angry." It's God's spin on the old adage, "Think before you speak."

As we consider what we'll feed our children today, let's also consider the words we'll use to nourish them. Let's offer up a balanced diet of encouragement, correction, instruction, affection, affirmation, and information. Let's provide a healthy verbal spread that will help and heal. After all, "Nothing is more appealing than speaking beautiful, life-giving words. For they release sweetness to our souls and inner healing to our spirits" (Proverbs 16: 24 TPT).

Dear Lord, slow down my tongue. Help me become more aware of what I'm saying before I say it—then give me wisdom to choose whether to speak, edit what I want to say, or keep my mouth shut. Amen.

A TIP TO TRY: Give your children words to treasure. Hide love notes in their lunch box or backpack, write on the bathroom mirror (Crayola Washable Window Markers work well), or send them a text during the day. Be sincere and specific in your message of love and encouragement.

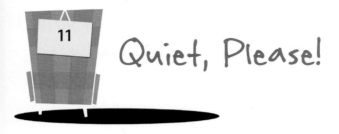

# Quiet, Please!

Surrender your anxiety!
Be silent and stop
your striving and you will
see that I am God.

—PSALM 46:10 TPT

It's common knowledge that a gift most moms would love to receive is a little peace and quiet. What isn't as widely known is that this particular gift benefits the whole family. Too much noise is stressful on everyone. It raises the cortisol levels in our bodies, which puts us into "fight or flight" mode. This means our bodies never actually relax. They're always on high alert. This can adversely affect our sleep patterns, blood pressure, anxiety level, and weight.

What's more, when we're emotionally exhausted (and

what mother isn't during demanding stages of our children's lives?), we become even more sensitive to noise. This is why even good sounds, like kids giggling or running as they play, can push us over an edge we didn't even realize we were approaching. As for our kids, a recent study has shown that those who grow up in noisy homes struggle with difficulties such as delayed language skills, increased anxiety, less cognitive growth, and impaired resilience.*

So let's hear it for peace and quiet! Let's do what we can to see that it has a place in our homes and in our hearts. Some of us have become so accustomed to the sound of chatter, video games, music, and TV in the background that silence is uncomfortable. Perhaps that's because silence makes it easier for us to hear the whisper of the Holy Spirit, who often clues us in to what's really going on inside ourselves.

The earlier we acquaint our kids with set quiet times throughout the day, the easier it will be for our home to become a place of peace, refuge, and spiritual insight, as well as ruckus celebration. We need both to lead a balanced life.

---

* Elizabeth Scott, "Stress and Noise Pollution," *Verywell*, June 30, 2012, https:// www.verywell.com/stress-and-noise-pollution-how-you-may-be-at-risk -3145041.

Dear Lord, I want to clearly hear your Spirit as I go through my busy day. Teach me how to listen and help me become comfortable with silence, so I can pass that lesson on to my children. Amen.

A TIP TO TRY: Take the batteries out of toys that make noise. Save them for a rainy day when the kids could use something new to play with. After you put the batteries back in, voilà!—new toy!

# Room to Grow

When I was a child, I spoke and thought
and reasoned as a child. But when I grew up,
I put away childish things.

—1 CORINTHIANS 13:11 NLT

The word *smother* has a "mother" right in the middle of it. Is that you? That will depend on how closely you choose to cling to your children as they mature. We all need a bit of room if we're going to grow. Just look at a newborn. You may adore the pint-sized pink footie she wore home from the hospital, but one day you're going to have to cast that cute little smock aside and dress her in a bigger size. Trying to squeeze your child into something she's outgrown is not only uncomfortable for her, but will eventually cause the garment to split at the seams, ruining the very outfit you cherish.

Obviously, it's the child, not the outfit, that really matters. And with motherhood, it's the child, not the experience of being a mother, that matters most. We may love being snuggled, holding our child's hand, and feeling needed as we protect our precious little one from the big bad world, but eventually, we have to let go of our child's hand and allow her to walk on her own. We have to risk letting her fall, letting her explore, and even giving her a bit of a nudge, if needed, to help her leave the nest as she approaches adulthood.

As our children mature, so should we. This means giving them, as well as ourselves, room to grow, to try new things, to fail, to succeed, and to discover who we are apart from one another. It may not always be easy, but it's the way God's designed us to grow up, grow wise, and grow strong.

Dear Lord, you know how deeply I love my children. Give me the courage to stretch the boundaries I've set as they grow. Give me peace, as I know you're holding them close, even when they're out of my reach. Amen.

A TIP TO TRY: Sometimes, opening the packaging for a Christmas or birthday gift can require a pair of scissors. Instead of opening your young children's gifts for them, hand them a pair of nail clippers and let them work on opening it themselves.

# Making the Miles Count

The LORD has given us eyes to see with
and ears to listen with.

—PROVERBS 20:12 GNB

Busy moms usually spend a lot of time in the car. Either we're running errands, navigating car pools, or battling rush hour. Every so often, we may even find ourselves enjoying the mixed blessing of a family road trip. Whatever road we're traveling, our kids are often in the car with us, which means travel time isn't wasted time; it's an opportunity to learn something new about our precious traveling companions.

When we're stuck in close quarters with someone, we have a choice: we can either get on each other's nerves or get to know each other better. Let's choose the latter. To do that, we need to be intentional. Before we get behind the wheel and our minds drift into autopilot as we navigate traffic, let's come up with a plan on how we'll connect.

Instead of turning on the radio, play a game, such as 20 Questions, license-plate bingo, or I spy. Even a short errand affords time to ask conversational questions, such as: "If you could have any super power, which one would it be?"; "What question would you most like to ask God?"; or "What do you like best about yourself?" Every time you buckle your seat belts, make asking one question a family tradition.

As children get older, car pools are also a prime time to learn more about them and their friends. Kids seem to forget a silent driver is listening, as they candidly share information about themselves and their day. This is a great time to pay attention to their conversation, as well as the road.

As we become more intentional about our travel time, we'll find that with every mile we put on our car, we'll travel a bit further in our relationship with those we love.

Dear Lord, help me not go on autopilot when I get behind the wheel. Help me be a better, more considerate driver and find creative ways to connect with my kids along the road. Amen.

A TIP TO TRY: Wrap inexpensive toys and treats before long car trips. After every rest stop (once the kids are buckled in) hand them a surprise ... a candy necklace, an action figure, a granola bar, an inflatable ball, or a jar of bubble solution to be used at the next rest stop. It will make getting back on the road easier and more enjoyable for everyone.

14

# A Cry for Help

I am worn out, O LORD; have pity on me!
Give me strength; I am completely exhausted
and my whole being is deeply troubled.
How long, O LORD, will you wait to help me?

—PSALM 6:2–3 GNB

Some days are more than a mother's heart can bear. Yes, you're exhausted. Yes, your kids seem snarkier than usual. Yes, the house is beginning to look like an episode of a hoarding reality show. But there's more. The evening news reports yet another tragedy, one that seemed to be unthinkable—until it became reality. Or perhaps the news hits much closer to home. It's a loss, a diagnosis, a betrayal that you never saw coming, but it's arrived. You find yourself paralyzed, unable to care for yourself. How are you supposed to care for your kids?

When your sorrow's so deep you can't hear God's voice through the pain, when you no longer sense God's presence, leaving you feeling lost and alone, when you're unsure where to turn for help … stop. Close your eyes for just a moment. Sit quietly and remember, "The LORD is close to the brokenhearted; he rescues those whose spirits are crushed" (Psalm 34:18 NLT). Just because we feel emotionally disconnected from God, doesn't mean he isn't near. We're like young children playing peek-a-boo. Even when a veil of sadness obscures our view, God remains right where he's always been—by our side. We'd never abandon our own children, especially in their time of need. Would we expect our heavenly Father to do any less?

Take a moment to cry out to God, even if the only word you can muster is, "Help!" Then risk reaching out a bit further and let others know you're hurting and need help: family, friends, neighbors, a pastor, or counselor—anyone God brings to mind. Often God provides the answer to our prayers through the people he's brought into our lives.

Dear Lord, even when I'm at a loss for words, you know what's on my heart. Please comfort me with peace and a sense of your presence. Amen.

A TIP TO TRY: Start a Prayer Text Circle with friends. Text a prayer anytime, anywhere, when your heart is heavy or filled with praise, and when possible, each person in the circle will stop to pray as soon as they receive a text. Then, they will text back a short prayer or word of encouragement.

# Dressed to Bless

Charm can be misleading, and beauty is vain
and so quickly fades, but this virtuous woman
lives in the wonder, awe, and fear of the Lord.
She will be praised throughout eternity.

—Proverbs 31:30 tpt

It started when we were just kids. We treated our mother's closet as our fantasy wardrobe, slathered on her lipstick, and tried walking in her heels. We primped and preened, dressed up our baby doll, and dreamed of the day we'd be a mom in real life.

That day is finally here. Now we have a living, breathing baby doll that we can dress anyway we want. We can even fill our closet with our very own fantasy wardrobe, if finances allow. In a sense, we're still playing dress-up, still trying our best to be beautiful and ensure that our children look cute. However, contrary to the popular adage, clothes do not make the man—or the mom or child, for that matter. Yes, they can influence a first impression, but so can a warm smile, friendly greeting, and genuine interest in those around us.

The more time, money, and effort we spend on trying to make ourselves and our children physically attractive, the more importance we place on appearance. Is that really the lesson we want to teach?

As they grow, our children will receive plenty of pressure from the media and their peers about how they should look and what they should wear. We can help balance that lopsided message in three ways: (1) by curbing our own impulse to shop for new clothes when we really don't need anything, (2) by refusing to make negative comments about our own appearance (including our weight), and (3) by complimenting our children (and others) more on the beauty of their inner qualities rather than their physical appearance.

Regardless of our age, our weight, or the cut of our clothes, if our heart is filled with faith, joy, and love, we can't help but grow more beautiful over time.

Dear Lord, everything you've created is beautiful in its own way. Help me learn to better appreciate the beauty you've woven into me, from the inside out. Amen.

A TIP TO TRY: The larger the wardrobe, the more time consuming it is for kids (as well as moms) to get ready in the morning. Help young children dress in record time by putting outfits together beforehand. Bundle together a shirt, pants, underwear, and socks with a hair tie or sturdy rubber band. Only keep a week's worth of outfits in your children's "dress myself" drawer at one time.

## 16

# Belief or Make-Believe?

Jesus responded, "Thomas, now that you've seen me, you believe. But there are those who have never seen me with their eyes but have believed in me with their hearts, and they will be blessed even more!"

—JOHN 20:29 TPT

When our kids have imaginary friends, we humor them. We attend tea parties with make-believe playmates or act as though stuffed animals are actually whispering secrets in our ear. After all, pretending is part of play. But when it comes to our relationship with God, do we believe he's really at work in our lives or are we playing a grown-up version of make-believe?

To Thomas, one of Jesus' followers, the Lord's resurrection certainly sounded like a fairy tale, and it's easy to understand why. A person who rises from the dead and walks out of a sealed tomb sounds more like best-selling fiction than fact. Only after Thomas saw Jesus in person did he acknowledge that what seemed like a fairy tale was honest-to-goodness real life.

So why do you believe? When have you seen evidence of God's hand at work? How has your faith made a tangible difference in your life? Can your children tell God is real by watching you?

If our children only hear about God on Sunday, church can seem like just another story time, and God another fairy tale. While pastors and Sunday school teachers can be wonderful mentors and examples for our children, it's our own personal faith that is their most influential classroom. The more diligent we are about spending time with God, especially through worship, prayer, and reading the Bible, the more aware we'll be of his presence and power—and the more aware our children will be of his reality in the world and in their lives.

Dear Lord, I want you to be the Lord of my life, not just a nice tradition that warms my heart. I long for the same to be true in my children's lives. Help our faith in you grow day by day. Amen.

A TIP TO TRY: Use dinnertime to nourish your children spiritually, as well as physically. Have each person ask one question about God that the rest of the family has to answer OR have each person share one thing they've experienced that day where they saw God at work in their lives or in the world around them.

## 17 Taken by Surprise

Now glory be to God, who by his mighty power at
work within us is able to do far more than we would
ever dare to ask or even dream of—infinitely beyond
our highest prayers, desires, thoughts, or hopes.

—Ephesians 3:20 tlb

There's a popular adage making the rounds that states,
"God will never give you more than you can handle."
Funny thing is, that sentiment isn't found anywhere in
Scripture. Some folks lean on 1 Corinthians 10:13 to
support the cliché, but that verse talks about how God
"will not let you be tempted beyond what you can bear."
Handling temptation is not the same thing as handling
struggles and hardship.

Just ask any mom whose child has colic or is diagnosed
with autism or cancer. Big or small, there are plenty of

things in this life that don't just push us to the edge, but right over it. If we could handle everything on our own, we'd be tempted to do just that: fly solo. Instead, difficult circumstances remind us of our own limits and help point us in the direction of our limitless God.

Consider Moses at the edge of the Red Sea with the Egyptian army close on his heels; Mary, Jesus' mother, when she realizes she's pregnant and unmarried; and Abraham when he's preparing to sacrifice his own beloved son (talk about facing more than one can handle!). But God helps each of these individuals write the next chapter of their story in a totally unexpected way.

We have an incredibly creative and powerful God who continues to take us by surprise. Yes, our hearts may still break; we may still wander in a proverbial desert for years; and we may not "handle" our circumstances, as much as wrestle with them, but through it all we have cause for hope. For when we are weak, our Lord is strong. We can do more together than we ever could on our own.

Dear Lord, life is overwhelming at times. Thank you for being there, for listening, for giving me hope, and for surprising me with joy, even in the midst of what feels like a dead end. I love you. Amen.

A TIP TO TRY: If your children catch a stomach bug, bring out the potty-training chair. Keep it near their bed, so they don't have to run to the bathroom when they're feeling sick. It's not only convenient, but easy to clean.

## 18 The Blessing of Buffering

With tender humility and quiet patience,
always demonstrate gentleness and
generous love toward one another,
especially toward those who may try your patience.

—Ephesians 4:2 TPT

You're running late, as usual. That's when your toddler spills a glass of milk on the floor, and your five-year-old decides that *today* is the day she's going to tie her shoes "all by myself." If you were a cartoon character, there'd be steam coming out of your ears.

But you're not a character—or a caricature—you're a busy mom, gifted by God with individuality and free will. You can blow your stack Looney Tune-style … or choose to practice patience. Which will it be?

Every child, whether compliant or a rebel at heart,

will test a parent's patience now and then. It's part of the process of growing up. It takes awhile to learn new skills, from holding a spoon to holding our tongue, and some of us may still be working on the latter, which serves to remind us that we not only need to practice patience with others (including our kids), but that others need to practice patience with us—except for God, of course. His patience doesn't need any practice. It's already endless and filled with grace.

As our own children help us master the art of patience, one way we can be proactive in the process is by allowing ourselves more margin in our schedule. Our patience will more likely wear thin if our day is overcommitted, and we're always running a bit behind. Building a buffer into each day allows extra time for unexpected traffic, teaching moments, mistakes, and the occasional meltdown. It also comes in handy when spontaneity strikes. Who knows when a celebratory ice cream cone might be exactly what's needed?

Dear Lord, thank you for your gift of time. Help me spend it well—not by trying to fit more into my day, but by being disciplined enough to allow myself and my family room to breathe. Amen.

A TIP TO TRY: Help your kids get into the habit of being early, rather than late. Anytime they're ready at least five minute *before* it's time to head out the door (set the alarm on your phone to keep it fair), put a penny in their Time Well Spent jar. (You may also want to fill an Early Box with books your kids can only read during those spare moments.) Let your kids spend their pennies any way they like.

## 19 Beyond Compare

Let everyone be devoted to fulfill the work God
has given them to do with excellence, and their joy
will be in doing what's right and being themselves,
and not in being affirmed by others.

—GALATIANS 6:4 TPT

Every mom feels her kids are beyond compare, but
that doesn't mean they won't be compared with others throughout their lives. Moments after our children
are born, they're weighed, measured, and given an Apgar
score. And that's just the beginning. Their first word, first
step, what size they wear, how well they read, or how fast
they run will all be measured against their peers. Chances
are good they'll not only be compared academically,
physically, and socially by teachers and physicians, but
also by so-called friends in locker room whispers and on

social media. In other words, our kids will have ample opportunities to feel as though they don't quite measure up in one area or another.

We understand how they feel. As moms, we compare ourselves (and feel others are evaluating us) in everything from how we discipline to how quickly we lose that "baby weight." Yet all of us, kids and moms included, truly are beyond compare. We were designed by God as a one-of-a-kind original.

Like unique pieces of a jigsaw puzzle, we each have a specific hole to fill in the big picture of life. Without each one of us, history would be incomplete. We can choose how well or poorly we fill the individual role we've been given, but even then, the only comparison we can make is to our own God-given potential.

So let's opt out of the rating game. Let's refuse to pit our children against each other by verbally comparing them to others or playing favorites. Let's celebrate our children's differences, as well as our own, for each one of us is unique and irreplaceable. Nothing can compare to that.

Dear Lord, help me get out of the habit of comparing myself or my children to others—for better or for worse. Allow me to celebrate each individual as your own unique masterpiece. Amen.

A TIP TO TRY: Make a jigsaw puzzle using a family portrait. (There are several photo websites that offer this option.) When you pray together as a family, have each person hold a piece as you pray. After you say amen, complete the puzzle as a family. Discuss how each piece fits together perfectly, like each person in your family.

## What's Really Mine?

The community of believers was one in heart
and mind. None of them would say, "This is mine!"
about any of their possessions,
but held everything in common.

—ACTS 4:32 CEB

There's nothing quite like the bond between siblings who both have their hands on the same toy. We can try cajoling, distracting, demanding, or attempting to physically pry the object from their sticky fingers, but until someone loosens his or her grip, it's a tug-of-war of wills—a battle that's been brewing since the day we were born.

*Mine* is a powerful word. Sometimes our battle is less about the object in question and more about our own selfish pride. Take the two mothers who stood before

King Solomon, each claiming the same baby as her own (1 Kings 3:16–28). When Solomon offered to divide the baby with a sword, giving half to each woman, only the real mother was willing to let go of her child to save the baby's life.

When we become laser focused on what we're afraid of losing (including our pride), we lose sight of what we have to gain. When our children won't share a toy, when we hesitate to allow a friend to borrow our new car, when we get angry with our spouse because he ate the last brownie (the one we'd deemed "mine" in our minds), what we're really sacrificing is community. We're putting stuff before people. We're forgetting that *community* comes from the word *communal*.

We're also forgetting that everything we possess is really ours only by the grace of God. Where we're born, who we're born to, our ability to work, think, and create—they're all gifts from our benevolent God. When we share with others, we reflect our heavenly Father's generosity, giving a bit of ourselves and our heart along with what we unselfishly extend to those around us.

Dear Lord, help me instill in my children the art of sharing, as I continue to master it myself. Thank you for every gift you give us, each and every day. Amen.

A TIP TO TRY: Need to clean and sanitize some of your tiny tykes' plastic possessions? Put them in a mesh laundry bag and run them through the dishwasher.

## 21 Put Yourself in Time-Out!

It is in vain that you rise up early
and go late to rest,
eating the bread of anxious toil;
for he gives to his beloved sleep.

—PSALM 127:2 ESV

For every child who refuses to take a nap, there's a mother, somewhere, wishing she could take it for him. Parenting can be exhausting—physically, mentally, and emotionally. We're on call 24 hours a day. There's no quitting time, vacation days, or sick leave. So what's a busy, burned-out mom to do?

God designed our bodies to need rest and relaxation on a regular basis. He also designed women to be able to become moms, which means there has to be a happy medium somewhere—a balance where we can take care of our kids as well as ourselves.

God, himself, provides an example. Genesis 1:31–2:2 tells us that after creating the world, "God looked at everything he had made, and it was very good … By the seventh day God finished the work he had been doing. So on the seventh day he rested from all his work" (ICB). What a gift it is to ourselves and to our children if we do the same!

Unlike creating the world, parenting isn't a job we can finish in under a week. To keep our energy and attitude at their best, we need to take regular breaks along the way. We need to feed ourselves healthy meals, get enough rest, schedule regular check-ups, and allow room in our busy week for play, praise, and reflection. Caring for our bodies not only provides us with a better quality of life, it's a way of giving thanks to the one who made them.

It's not selfish to help our children understand that Mom has needs, just as they do. It encourages them to lead a more balanced life in the future. If you feel your eyes getting heavy just reading these words, perhaps today is the day that lesson begins.

Dear Lord, for too long I've held running myself ragged as a hard-earned badge of motherhood. Teach me how to rest in your arms, caring for myself with the same tenderness I do my children. Amen.

A TIP TO TRY: Take the fight out of naptime for your preschoolers with a Quiet Time Fort. A small pop-up tent or a blanket over the dining table can be a hideaway where they read books or play with small toys quietly each afternoon for an hour. If they fall asleep, hurray! If not, you still get an hour of quiet—and maybe a chance for a bit of shut-eye for yourself.

## 22 All Together Now

> Children are a gift from the LORD;
> they are a real blessing.
>
> —PSALM 127:3 GNB

Ralph Waldo Emerson said, "It is a happy talent to know how to play."* We work hard to help our children cultivate this talent. We overstuff toy boxes, buy bigger game consoles, erect swing sets, and sign them up for soccer camps. Sure, we want our kids to enjoy themselves, but sometimes our unspoken goal is to keep them occupied.

We have important stuff to do: clean the kitchen, fold the laundry, or finish up that project we couldn't complete at work—and all of it is easier to do without kids underfoot. Yet perhaps we need to take a fresh look at

---

\* Ralph Waldo Emerson, *Emerson in His Journals* (Cambridge, MA: Harvard University Press, 1984), 138.

work and play. Our kids don't need toys as much as they need us to play with them.

Instead of handing them a coloring book, why not sit down and color with them? Watch a movie snuggled together, even if you know how it ends. Prepare a picnic lunch to eat in the backyard instead of simply sending them outside to play.

On the flip side, creatively transform some of the chores you do into games your kids can enjoy "playing" with you. For instance, have kids set the table for dinner, creating a unique centerpiece for the table each night. Fold laundry together by color, one child handling everything red, another folding blue. Or have a race to empty trashcans from around the house into a large communal container the night before trash is collected.

With the right attitude, even chores can be fun for everyone. As the Irish playwright George Bernard Shaw said, "We don't stop playing because we grow old; we grow old because we stop playing.[*] Perhaps playing and working right along with our kids is the secret to remaining young at heart.

---

[*] George Bernard Shaw, http://www.brainyquote.com/quotes/quotes/g/george bern120971.html.

Dear Lord, remind me to play with my kids, instead of simply handing them another toy to distract them until dinnertime. Help me to be young at heart and humble enough to take a lesson from my kids. Amen.

A TIP TO TRY: What were your favorite toys as a kid? Introduce your children to paper dolls, making and flying kites, card games like Go Fish, playing dress-up in your closet, or whatever your favorite pastimes were. Be sure to join in the fun!

23

# Chew on This

Taste and see that the LORD is good.
Oh, the joys of those who take refuge in him!
—PSALM 34:8 NLT

Picky eaters put a damper on dinnertime. Not only do they turn up their nose at food that's not on their limited "like" list, but they also refuse to try anything new. As a mom, it's frustrating to know that stubbornness, not taste buds, often dictate what our child is going to eat. Plus, if our child decides to shun an entire food group—such as vegetables—it can be tough to ensure he is getting the nutrition needed to thrive.

Perhaps God feels some of that same frustration when we pick and choose what Bible verses we're going to "like." We all have our favorites, such as John 3:16, Jeremiah 29:11, and Psalm 23. We like to snack on verses that emphasize God's love, grace, and purpose in our life. However, there are plenty of verses we find harder to swallow: ones that conflict with our view of God or ourselves, ones that ask us to do something hard or unpleasant, or ones that we simply can't comprehend.

God clearly tells us in Isaiah 55:9, "As the heavens are higher than the earth, so are my ways higher than your ways and my thoughts than your thoughts." We're never going to fully understand God—or even his Word, but it doesn't mean we should stop tasting and trying to digest who God is and what he's said to us through Scripture.

The Bible is a balanced meal, from creation in Genesis to Christ's return in Revelation. Picking and choosing what we're going to believe, act on, and ignore is like eating dessert while leaving our entree untouched. Let's refuse to be picky spiritual eaters. Instead, let's risk tasting truths that challenge us. The more of God and his Word we take into our lives, the better moms we'll be.

Dear Lord, I long to hear from you, but so often forget to spend time reading the words you've already given me. Help me develop a taste and a hunger for your Word. Amen.

A TIP TO TRY: Unsure where to get started reading the Bible? Starting with page one can be a tough way to begin. Instead, start by reading a chapter of the Gospels (Matthew, Mark, Luke, and John) each day, and then move on to the Psalms. From there, challenge yourself to read through the Bible in a year (you can find a plan online). Throughout the day, ask God to continue to speak to you through what you've read.

## 24

# We Are Family

God decided in advance to adopt us
into his own family by bringing us to himself
through Jesus Christ. This is what he wanted to do,
and it gave him great pleasure.

—Ephesians 1:5 nlt

Statistics tell us the average American family has 1.87 children. How many families do you know with one-eighth of a child? The word *average* may serve us well in terms of research, but it cannot accurately describe real life.

Every family has its own singular blueprint—a unique blend of individuals in relationship with one another. We may have become a mother by giving birth or welcomed a child in through adoption, foster care, or as a stepchild. Regardless of how we all wound up together, we are family; and what a beautiful bond that can be.

Consider God's own family. What a crazy quilt of adopted individuals! Some people become God's children when they're literally children, which is often true of those raised in a Christian home. Others come to God later in life, led to a living faith through a friend, a message at church, reading God's Word, or countless other avenues God uses so creatively in our lives. It doesn't matter how we became children of God. It only matters that we are.

The same is true with our own children. What matters is we're in this thing called "life" together. Like the Three Musketeers, we long to be "all for one and one for all." So what can we do to make the word *family* more precious in our children's eyes and ours?

We can honor each individual with our words and refuse to make one member the butt of family jokes in public or in private. We can serve, respect, and support each other through loving actions. We can pray for our family both together and as individuals. And, we can assure our children that we have their back through our words and our actions. Remember that when we work together as a family, we are stronger as a whole than we are as individuals.

Dear Lord, help me grasp the true sanctity of family. Show me how to help bind each member of my family closer to each other and to you. Amen.

A TIP TO TRY: Make a personalized family crest. Have each person come up with a symbol for a unique gift they believe they add to the family and incorporate those symbols into your own coat of arms. Find a creative way to display your crest in your home.

# Prime Time

> Stop imitating the ideals and opinions of the culture
> around you, but be inwardly transformed by the Holy
> Spirit through a total reformation of how you think.
> This will empower you to discern God's will as you
> live a beautiful life, satisfying and perfect in his eyes.
>
> —ROMANS 12:2 TPT

There's an honorary member of our family who doesn't even have a name, but who we call on to be a babysitter, teacher, entertainer, and friend to our children. According to StatisticBrain.com, 54 percent of kids would rather spend time with this family companion than with their very own dad—that's the kind of influence that should make us sit up and take notice. Can you guess who this influential family member is? That's right, it's the television.

The television is a tool, not a parent or playmate. When used with a bit of restraint and forethought, it can provide information, entertainment, and laughter for our family. But when we cease to be intentional about what we watch, it can also allow an unrealistic and ungodly view of life into our home. Sitcoms, commercials, romantic comedies, graphic sex, and violence—they're all fodder for our mind, influencing how we think about our appearance, money, intimacy, the world, the opposite sex, and God. Even the witty banter of our favorite sitcoms can shape what we believe is an acceptable way to speak and treat one another.

We don't need to hide ourselves in a protective bubble to live in a way that's pleasing to God, but we need to be aware of what we're allowing to influence the way we think. Is cable playing a bigger role in transforming our mind and our children's minds than God's Spirit? Let's be honest about the role TV plays in our home. It may sound prudish, but one way to begin is to pray for wisdom when you sit down in front of the TV. If God's Spirit nudges you to change the channel or turn it off, that is one voice always worth listening to in prime time.

Dear Lord, please provide me with wisdom and honesty as I rethink what part TV plays in our home. I want my mind to be shaped and transformed by you. Please help me understand my part in that process. Amen.

A TIP TO TRY: Be intentional about turning on the TV. Make a schedule of what you're going to watch in the coming week. After each show, have a TV Talk. Keep it brief and light. As a family, evaluate what was positive and negative and discuss what kind of review you think God would give the show.

## 26 Mental Gymnastics

Don't be pulled in different directions or worried about a thing. Be saturated in prayer throughout each day, offering your faith-filled requests before God with overflowing gratitude. Tell him every detail of your life, then God's wonderful peace that transcends human understanding, will make the answers known to you through Jesus Christ.

—PHILIPPIANS 4:6–7 TPT

Worry is the Olympian of mental gymnastics. It goes around and around on the uneven bars of our psyche, twisting, turning, and escalating our anxiety by threatening that we're going to lose it all. It doesn't play fair. It blows things out of proportion, contorting lies into truth and truth into doubt. It can keep us up at night, mess with our digestion, and immobilize us with fear.

What's worse is it's often equated with love. It's implied that the more a mom worries about her kids, the more she cares, which is just another lie worry likes to tell. Worry doesn't do anything more than keep our mental wheels spinning on overdrive. It doesn't change anything, fix anything, or help our children or us in any way.

So what can we do to cut this destructive routine short? The only way we actually win the gold is by letting go. If worry is a habit we've been perfecting for years, it's going to take a while to learn how to "stick the landing."

First, we have to recognize when our mind starts spinning. Once we do, we can immediately redirect our train of thought toward God. By telling God what we're worried about, we transform our concerns into prayers. Next, we ask for wisdom, so we can discern what we have control over and what we don't. Finally, we act. We do what can be done, and whatever is out of our hands we put gratefully into God's.

It's only natural to check back with God now and then, to make sure he's still holding what we cannot, but every time we do, let's voice our trust in Him, adding a word of thanks. He's bigger than our worries, and through him, we can be too.

Dear Lord, you know my every concern, and you care about them all, big and small. Please give me perspective, wisdom, and the courage to let go. Thank you for helping me stop worry in its tracks. Amen.

A TIP TO TRY: Keep a Worry Jar on the kitchen counter. Have your kids write their worries on a piece of wafer paper (made of rice or potatoes and sold at craft stores.) Every evening, empty the jar and pray together over the concerns. Then, put the "worries" in water and watch the paper dissolve, just as God dissolves our worries.

# Sibling Rivalry

When Joseph's brothers saw him coming,
they recognized him in the distance.
As he approached, they made plans to kill him.
—Genesis 37:18 NLT

Unlike Joseph's eleven brothers, chances are pretty good that your kids have probably never thrown a sibling into a pit or sold them into slavery, but that doesn't mean they haven't occasionally wished a sibling were no longer part of the family. Jealousy, gender differences, selfishness, immaturity, a sense of competition, or volatile temperaments can all open the door to conflict between siblings—even brothers and sisters who really do love each other.

What can we do to help our children get along? First, we can refuse to act like Joseph's father. Jacob very visibly played favorites, singling out Joseph from his brothers and giving him a flashy multicolored coat. Even if we feel a stronger affinity for one child over another—perhaps because that child is more compliant or shares interests or talents we hold in high regard—love doesn't play favorites.

It isn't possible to treat all of our kids equally, but we can treat them equitably. We can do our best to be fair and just, trying to express our love and pride for each in the way they respond to most favorably. We can also do our best to prevent one child from controlling the entire family. This is tough when one child consistently gets in trouble or has heightened physical, mental, or emotional needs. In this situation, we need to be more vigilant than usual to make certain our other children don't feel lost in the shuffle.

One thing we can do to make each child feel special is to schedule one-on-one time together. We can also encourage our children to pray for one another. It's hard to be angry with someone you're talking to God about on a regular basis.

Dear Lord, thank you for my children, as well as my own siblings. Give me the wisdom and perseverance I need to keep these family ties from getting twisted up in knots. Amen.

A TIP TO TRY: Privately, recruit each of your children for the Secret Service. Explain that their job is to serve a specific sibling in secret. They can make a gift, do a chore, or find a unique way to honor, encourage, or entertain their brother or sister—without allowing him or her to discover who's behind the thoughtful gesture.

28

# Rash Guard

Spouting off before listening
to the facts is both shameful and foolish.
—Proverbs 18:13 NLT

As busy moms, jumping to conclusions may be the only exercise we practice on a regular basis. After all, if we feel we know others well, it's tempting to act before we've heard all of the facts. It seems like an expedient way to solve a problem.

That is exactly how Joseph wound up in prison (Genesis 39:1–21). Potiphar trusted Joseph to manage his entire household, but when the "well-built and handsome" Joseph spurned the advances of Potiphar's wife, she took revenge by accusing Joseph of trying to seduce her. Potiphar took the bait. Potiphar had known his wife longer than Joseph, and he expected her to be truthful and faithful—but she wasn't. And Joseph was the one who paid a steep price.

Though the stakes are smaller than winding up in prison when dealing with our own kids, it doesn't mean ill-informed assumptions won't have consequences. When we find a broken lamp in the living room, we may automatically shout out the name of our "rowdy" child, but our mild-mannered child could be responsible, or one of the neighbor kids who came over to play, or the cat. If we act before we know the whole story, we may wind up breaking a little heart instead of solving the mystery of a broken lamp.

Just because one scenario is more likely than another doesn't make it true. The more we assume we know how a person will react, what they'll say, or what they'll do in a given situation, the more we squeeze them into a mold in our mind. We profile them. But people are constantly changing, growing, and maturing. Let's give them room to exercise their free will, as we exercise restraint in holding back our judgment until all of the facts are in.

Dear Lord, slow me down enough to help me really listen when people speak, including my kids. Help me break any tendencies I have to finish their sentences or make rash judgments. Amen.

A TIP TO TRY: Would-be thieves will jump to the wrong conclusion if you try this trick. When your family is at the beach or the pool, wrap valuables (such as your car keys and cell phones) in a disposable diaper and set it with your towels. Voilà!—virtually theft proof!

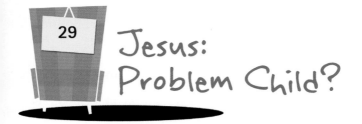

# Jesus: Problem Child?

His parents didn't know what to think.
"Son," his mother said to him, "why have you done
this to us? Your father and I have been frantic,
searching for you everywhere."

—LUKE 2:48 NLT

You'd think being the mother of a sinless son would be trouble free, but no. Even Jesus drove his earthly parents crazy—at least once. When he was twelve, he accompanied his parents and relatives on a trip to Jerusalem, but when they all headed home, Jesus stayed behind to converse with the teachers in the temple. Three days later, his panicked parents finally located him.

Imagine how you'd feel if God's Son was entrusted to you—and you *lost* him! Then imagine what you'd say if your own preteen wandered off for a couple of days without telling you. It probably wouldn't be pretty. Yet after being reprimanded once, the Bible tells us Jesus returned home with Mary and Joseph and "was obedient to them" (Luke 2:51). What follows in the next verse is every mother's dream: "And Jesus grew in wisdom and stature, and in favor with God and man."

One of the hardest parts about being a parent is dealing with discipline. Figuring out what our house rules are going to be and how we'll respond when they're broken is an ongoing process that matures right along with our children. And to really keep you on your toes, what works with one child may not be effective with another.

While we're figuring it out—one day at a time—it's good to keep Luke 2:52 in mind, as it's really our ultimate goal. What can we do today to help our children grow wiser? To help them mature spiritually, relationally, and emotionally? How does discipline play a positive role in that process? That sounds like a prayer request worth repeating every day.

Dear Lord, every day is a challenge in this area. Please help me grow in wisdom along with my children, discerning willful disobedience from what's accidental. Help me respond in love, not anger, keeping Luke 2:52 in mind. Amen.

A TIP TO TRY: Instead of sending kids to time-out, where they simply sit and stew, give them a project to finish, such as stringing a set number of beads on a piece of yarn or completing a dot-to-dot worksheet or small jigsaw puzzle. It not only helps them calm down, but it refocuses their energy in a more positive direction.

# Focus on the Positive

My child, if your heart is wise,
my own heart will rejoice!
Everything in me will celebrate
when you speak what is right.

—Proverbs 23:15–16 NLT

Child development experts call it "positive reinforcement." However, celebrating the best in our kids works equally well. Regardless of what we call it, drawing attention to the things our children do right, rather than continually harping on what they do wrong, is better for all of us. It builds our children's confidence, reassures them of our love, and helps heal the wounds inflicted by all of the negative messages the world (and our children's own insecurities) bombards them with every day. It also helps us focus on the beauty God's woven into each of our children, instead of on their weaknesses and imperfections. A positive perspective overwrites liability with possibility.

Unconvinced? Which verse makes you feel more valued as a child of God: "God so loved the world that he gave his one and only Son, that whoever believes in him shall not perish but have eternal life" (John 3:16) or "The world continued to mess up so royally that God was forced to sacrifice his only child, and if those ungrateful people refuse to believe in him they'll die"? God chose the former to convey his care for us.

When our kids are going through difficult seasons, trying to find something positive to say can feel like an expert-level scavenger hunt, which means it's more important than ever for us to be looking for what's good and worthy of celebration in our children. Sincerity, not flattery, is our goal.

One way to redirect our own brains down a more positive track is to provide verbal "love notes" for our children. Complete open-ended sentences, such as, "I'm so glad you're part of this family, because_____" or "I was really proud of you today when _____." Who knows, your positive words may become love notes your children treasure right into adulthood.

Dear Lord, expose the beauty you've woven into each of my children more clearly to me. Help me celebrate who they are in a way that encourages them to become everything you desire them to be. Amen.

A TIP TO TRY: Give your kids positive rather than negative direction. For instance, "If you finish cleaning your room before the timer goes off in 15 minutes, we'll read a bedtime story together" instead of, "You won't get a bedtime story if you don't clean your room." Help your kids focus on what they *can* do, instead of what they can't.

# Rebel or Reformer?

Josiah was eight years old when he became king
of Judah. He did what was pleasing to the LORD;
he followed the example of his ancestor King David,
strictly obeying all the laws of God.

—2 CHRONICLES 34:1–2 GNB

God used a kid to turn the kingdom of Judah around. Not only that, but Josiah was a kid from a "bad" family. Both his father and grandfather were just two dishonorable examples in a long line of evil Jewish kings. Yet Josiah chose to follow in the godly footsteps of his mother, the prophet Jeremiah (who later became Josiah's mentor), and his ancestor King David, to become one of the great leaders of spiritual reform in Judah.

Who knows the impact our own children will have on the world in the years ahead? As moms, we have an impact on their lives right now. We have the opportunity to be a living lesson every day, a godly example of faith, love, and compassion.

However, being a great mom doesn't guarantee that our children will follow a noble path when they get older. God has given each of us many gifts, one of which is free will. Individually, we each choose what we will do with what we've been given, which means that even if we're fantastic moms, we can't take credit for everything our kids do right. And, if we make less than stellar choices, we're still not responsible for everything they do wrong.

Case in point, Josiah's own sons "did evil in the sight of the Lord" (2 Chronicles 36:1–8). They had an amazing example to follow, but they chose to use their free will to turn away from God, instead of drawing closer to him.

As moms, our prayers, loving actions, and positive example are not in vain. They all help provide our children with a solid foundation on which they can build a godly life. But it's up to them to choose what they'll create with all they've been given.

Dear Lord, please surround my children with wise, godly influences—and help me be one. Then, help them be strong enough to use their free will in ways that will make you (and me) smile. Amen.

A TIP TO TRY: Using blue painter's tape, make a "safe zone" around your barbecue, stove, or any areas you don't want your children to enter. Verbally reinforce that blue tape means "stop." The tape can't prevent a child from crossing over it, but it does provide a great visual warning.

# 32

# A Bounty of Blessing

"Give us today our daily bread."

—MATTHEW 6:11

Back in the "good old days" of Exodus, when the Israelites wandered through the wilderness for forty years, no one bugged Mom by asking, "What's for dinner?" The answer was always the same. "Manna." No fuss, no muss … no choices. But, today we're surrounded by an overabundance of decisions when it comes to feeding our family. We not only have to consider our nutritional needs but weigh it against what we have time to make, what we can afford, what's wilting in the fridge, what new recipe we saw on social media, and what our children will actually eat. Sometimes the monotony of manna sounds like a blessing.

Preparing nutritious, varied, kid-pleasing meals can be

a challenge when our schedule is tight. Plus the fact that food is often accompanied by its own set of emotional baggage can make mealtimes feel even more like a chore. But at its heart, food is simply fuel; we need it to live. Period. Everything else is window dressing.

During the harried days of early motherhood, simple is best. It's okay to serve sandwiches, oatmeal, or yogurt parfaits for dinner every now and then. Do your best to prevent the dinner table from becoming a battlefield. Always offer at least one dish you know your kids will eat. Encourage them to have as many servings as they like but only take what they can eat. They may only eat bananas or mashed potatoes one night, but it will all even out over time.

If there's no power struggle or pressure on you to perform, dinner together can become a highlight of each day—a time to relax, reconnect, and be thankful our table holds more than a manna buffet.

Dear Lord, I never want to take the food you've provided for granted. Help me be more aware of what a life-giving blessing it is as I shop for it, cook it, serve it, and even clean up after it. Amen.

A TIP TO TRY: Kid-friendly tapas make mealtime a bite-sized delight. Serve a variety of tasty treats to each child in an ice cube tray (you can even sneak in leftovers). Single-bite servings eaten with fingers, toothpicks, or tiny demitasse spoons is less overwhelming for small children than a plate of food—and a lot more fun!

33

# No Excuses

"You know with all your heart and soul that not one of all the good promises the LORD your God gave you has failed. Every promise has been fulfilled."

—JOSHUA 23:14

When kids make a promise, it can be quite a production. They cross their heart, pinky swear, or even prick their finger to show how serious they are about vowing to keep a secret. Why all of the dramatics? Perhaps it's because children figure out at an early age that people don't always follow through on what they say they'll do.

Are we one of those people? Even a mom with the best of intentions can become a promise breaker. Sometimes we voice our wishes instead of our plans; for instance, our kids ask to visit the zoo and we say, "Not today, maybe next weekend," but what we really mean is, "That sounds like fun sometime." Or, maybe we promise the moon, when we can only deliver Pluto; for example, assuring our kids, "This'll only take five minutes," when we know it's bound to take twenty.

When we exaggerate, tell half-truths, or outright lie just to try and keep our kids happy right now, we're setting them up for disappointment later. We're also teaching them that our words—which they may interpret as our love—cannot be trusted.

Yes, the unexpected happens. Unlike God, there may be a promise we're unable to fulfill on occasion. But when that happens, we apologize, assure our children they're important to us, and let them know we're disappointed too. If a broken promise is an exception instead of the rule, it won't shake the foundation of our children's trust in us.

Let's refuse to cross our proverbial fingers behind our backs. Whether it's a promise to go to the zoo or that this is the last time we're going to ask them to come inside before there are consequences, let's be promise keepers. Let's mean what we say and say what we mean.

Dear Lord, thank you for being so faithful to me, for fulfilling every promise you've made, and for being worthy of my trust. Show me how to be worthy of my children's trust in words and deed. Amen.

A TIP TO TRY: Make a weekly or monthly calendar for your children. Once something is on the calendar, it's a promise. If it isn't written down, then it's just a maybe. This can include everything from a trip to the park, to reading two books before bedtime tomorrow night because you're too busy to read one aloud tonight.

## 34 Everything in Its Place

He counts the stars
and calls them all by name.
—Psalm 147:4 nlt

Are you one of those moms born with all-purpose cleanser in your veins? Are your spices alphabetized, your freezer organized, and your closets color coordinated? Can you french-braid your daughter's hair with one hand tied behind your back? If so, consider today your day off. It may be tough to sit back and read a book while dust mites threaten to land on your settee, but sometimes, too much of a good thing ceases to be a good thing. Learning to sit still, breathe, and enjoy the presence of God (even when dishes remain in the sink) is even more important than being able to see your reflection in the lids of your saucepans.

However, if your home looks like it's been pillaged by pirates (and you couldn't care less), it's time to get things under control. The busier we are the more important organization becomes to help provide breathing room in our lives. Still, if you were born without a methodical bone in your body, don't despair. Organization is a skill that can be acquired with a bit of prayer, resolve, and self-discipline.

If we look at our Father's world, we see his organizational skills run deep. Plants grow, bear fruit, drop seeds, die, become compost, and aid in the growth of new plants. Planets keep revolving around the sun. Atoms hold together. Life goes on. Having an organized plan really does keep the world spinning round.

Within the little world of our very own home, we, including every member of our family, have a responsibility to bring order out of chaos. It relieves stress, saves time, enables us to take better care of the resources God's given us—and makes our home feel like a refuge of blessing, instead of another burden.

Dear Lord, thank you for the home you've provided for us. Guide me in knowing what to do and what to leave undone each day. Amen.

A TIP TO TRY: Break big jobs down into smaller manageable jobs for yourself, as well as your kids. Instead of trying to organize the whole kitchen, start with one drawer or your spice rack. When you finish, celebrate what you've accomplished, and then tackle the next little corner that could use your help.

# Mother's Little Helper

Some of you say, "We can do anything we want to."
But I tell you that not everything is good for us.
So I refuse to let anything have power over me.

—1 CORINTHIANS 6:12 CEV

We label them stress relievers, energy boosters, or a way to unwind. It's how we treat ourselves after a hard day with the kids. We've earned it, right? But sometimes the way we treat ourselves is actually hurting us, instead of helping us. How can we tell? By how tightly our "little helpers" have a hold over our heart.

Caffeine, shopping, a glass of wine, a sugary snack, binge-watching TV, sleep aids—even exercise—are only a few of the more common indulgences we moms choose to help us relax. However, when we become more comfortable indulging in private, our treats become guilty pleasures, and there's really nothing pleasurable about guilt. Guilt is God's alarm system, warning us we're headed in the wrong direction. If we're hesitant for others to know how frequently we rely on our little helpers, then that hesitance should alert us to that fact that our indulgence has crossed over into more of an addiction; meaning it has power over us.

Or perhaps, we don't indulge alone. We enjoy that third glass of wine at Mom's Night Out or a second helping of dessert at the church potluck because everyone is encouraging us to do just that. Friends who cajole us into not feeling guilty about crossing a line we know isn't healthy are not really friends. They're using us as co-conspirators to help drown out their own feelings of guilt.

It's time to start paying attention to who's in control of our lives. If it's getting harder and harder to say no to something, it's time to say yes to breaking a bad habit. That's the best way to treat ourselves—by using the freedom God's given us to choose the very best in life.

Dear Lord, I don't want to be ruled by anything in my life, other than a whole-hearted desire to seek and follow your will. Please give me the clarity and strength I need to do exactly that. Amen.

A TIP TO TRY: Is there any habit you find yourself leaning on a bit too heavily? Give it up for a week or a month. How does just the thought of setting it aside for awhile make you feel? Those feelings are a good indicator of how "addicted" you are. A further indication is how often you think about your favored indulgence the first day you just say no.

36

A True Gem

A truly good wife is the most
precious treasure a man can find!

—Proverbs 31:10 CEV

We've heard the phrase before: A good woman is hard to find. Perhaps it's because so many of us are buried in a pile of laundry while wearing a shirt covered in baby spit-up. It's like maternal camouflage! It can also lead us to believe that romance is a thing of the past.

When our days of wine and roses morph into whines and runny noses, it's tempting to allow our role as mom to supersede our role as wife, but motherhood (at least the hands-on part) lasts for only a season. Hopefully, our relationship with our husband will last until death do us part.

However, a marriage that lasts doesn't just happen. It takes commitment and effort on both sides: husband

and wife. We can encourage our husband in his role by being committed to doing well in our own, which means nurturing the love, friendship, and intimacy we shared as newlyweds, until it becomes a way of life instead of a nostalgic memory.

The best way to care for our children's needs is to make certain our own are being taken care of as well. Yes, we need "me time," but, we also need "we time" just with our spouse. We need to share conversations and experiences that help us rediscover the champion, companion, and lover in each other that first drew us together. We don't need to spend a lot of money, but we do need to spend some of our limited, valuable time. The returns we'll receive on our investment will continue paying dividends to us and our children for decades to come.

Dear Lord, please use my spouse to soften out rough places in my own character. Help me to refuse to keep score, instead treating him with grace, patience, generosity, and love. Amen.

A TIP TO TRY: Start an "It's a Date" bowl in your bedroom. Have both spouses write ideas for activities to do together on slips of paper and continually add them to the bowl. Include expensive dream dates and getaways, as well as inexpensive or free activities. Draw an idea from the bowl once a week and at least make plans to make it happen!

# 37 Carpe Diem Goes Digital

This is the day that the LORD has made;
let us rejoice and be glad in it.

—PSALM 118:24 ESV

Your baby girl is taking her first steps; your twins are giggling over putting their toes in the ocean for the very first time; it's your son's first game as quarterback on the high school football team—and where are you? You're watching it through the screen of your cell phone, recording it all so you can rewatch that amazing moment any time you want, along with your friends and family on social media, which is a good thing because you're missing the actual moment right now!

Believe it or not, Horace (who lived during the time of Augustus) has something to say about that. The phrase "carpe diem" first appears in a lyrical ode written by the

Roman poet. It's actually one small part of a phrase that is translated, "pluck the day, trusting as little as possible in the next one."

Plucking the day isn't synonymous with seizing it digitally so we can view it at a later date, when it's more convenient. It's more about grabbing it "now" with both hands. To do that, we have to put down our phone, stop updating social media, and savor this moment with our family—firsthand—instead of with the entire world.

It may go against the grain of today's digitally obsessed culture, but our family's story is not a reality show; it's reality. It's the one and only life we get to live. Our children will never be this age again and neither will we. Why waste this amazing moment posing for selfies in front of the Ferris wheel? Let's get on it and thank God for the joy of the ride!

Dear Lord, please help me break my need for the approval of others, especially when it comes to posting pictures and videos of my family. Help me wholly grasp the joy of this moment without having to post it. Amen.

A TIP TO TRY: Get in the habit of counting your blessings more than your "likes" on Facebook. On your next family vacation, refrain from posting anything. Only take photos you're going to put in an album or on the wall of your home. Focus on enjoying this time with your children instead of trying to fit all of your faces into a selfie.

38 Peacemaker Mom

If it is possible, as far as it depends on you,
live at peace with everyone.

—ROMANS 12:18

It's like an all-mom boxing match: homeschool vs. public school, breastfeeding vs. formula, cloth diapers vs. disposable. From pregnancy right through grandparenting, moms often have opposing views as to what's the best way to raise our kids.

It's good to be well-informed, to listen to opposing viewpoints, and to use critical thinking to help determine how we'll raise our kids, and why we'll raise them in that particular way. But when we feel so strongly about our decisions that we can't abide other moms coming to a conclusion different than our own, it's time to call a time-out before a discussion turns into a knock-down, drag-out fight.

Parenting isn't a math problem where we plug in the numbers and get the same answer every time we work the equation. It's more like painting a masterpiece— one that's never finished! There are so many variables involved; there's a unique child with a unique mother in a unique family at a unique time in history living in unique circumstances. And every mom with more than one kid knows that what works with one child isn't guaranteed to work equally well with a sibling. Talk about complex!

So let's call a truce before the fight gets started. If another mom challenges your parenting, don't get defensive; get inquisitive. Ask questions, such as: "What convinced you to make this choice?" "What challenges have you faced regarding it?" "What do you see as the main advantage in doing things this way?" Make sure to listen carefully, applaud what you can, share your opinion when invited, be humble enough to rethink a thing or two, and if your pride gets hurt along the way, try not to let your diaper bag get in a wad. Winning an argument is never worth losing a friend.

Dear Lord, you are the Prince of Peace. I want to walk in your footsteps. Please help me build other mothers up, instead of tearing them down—especially when there's a difference of opinion. Amen.

A TIP TO TRY: Help your children become critical thinkers and gracious conversationalists by holding a weekly Debate Night at the dinner table. Pick a controversial, kid-friendly topic, take turns debating differing sides of the issue, and discuss how to listen and disagree with respect.

# 39

# Messy Me

"Since you are children of a perfect Father in heaven,
you are to be perfect like him."
—MATTHEW 5:48 TPT

What every mother wants and needs in her life is more pressure, right? As if we don't already feel as though our spouse, kids, friends, neighbors, parents, in-laws (not to mention, ourselves!) feel that we should be like Mary Poppins, who's "practically perfect in every way," here's Jesus verbalizing that very same message. Or is he?

In our minds, we equate perfection with success and godliness. We picture a perfect house, perfectly decorated and immaculately kept; being the perfect weight for our height; and making meals that are perfectly balanced nutritionally, as well as delicious, economical, and consumed with enthusiasm by our entire family. We strive to make certain our budget balances, our birthday wishes are never belated, and our child is a miniature Mother Teresa when it comes to sharing toys with her friends. Yes, perfectionism is alive and well, especially in the mind of a mom who feels she doesn't quite measure up.

While the pressure we feel to be perfect may be real or imagined, one thing is certain: that pressure isn't coming from God. The word *perfect* in this passage of Scripture is actually the Greek word *teleioi*, which is also translated as "complete, whole, mature." Jesus isn't encouraging our tendencies toward perfectionism; he's telling us to act our age. And in the context of this passage, he's emphasizing that our love for one another should be like God's—wholly complete and mature.

So let's grow up and love well. Let's refuse to allow our fear of not measuring up hold us back any longer. Perfectionism isn't a motivation to help us be "better" moms; it's a distraction that keeps us from concentrating on what matters most.

Dear Lord, please reveal when I'm striving for a goal that isn't your will and isn't worth my time. Help me cast off false guilt and celebrate that your acceptance isn't based on what I do, but who I am— yours. Amen.

A TIP TO TRY: Help kids enjoy a bit of messy play without stressing out over cleaning up. Add a few drops of food color to a small amount of plain yogurt and put it in a freezer-sized Ziplock bag. Seal it carefully! Then, lay it flat on the kitchen floor or table and allow kids to "finger paint" mess-free by "drawing" on the outside of the bag with their fingertips.

# 40 One Step at a Time

Blessed are those whose strength is in you,
whose hearts are set on pilgrimage.

—PSALM 84:5

Motherhood is a journey. That being said, it certainly isn't one that follows a straight path. Instead of a superhighway, it feels more like a labyrinth. Walking in a labyrinth takes you through multiple twists and turns, sometimes leading you so close to where you've already been that it feels as though you're not making any progress at all. But you are. You're always moving closer toward the center.

Labyrinths became popular in the twelfth century. Before that time, people often went on pilgrimages to Jerusalem in an effort to draw closer to God. However, the Crusades made a journey to the Holy Land dangerous and often inaccessible, so these patterned pathways were designed as a mini-pilgrimage. Participants would meditate on drawing closer to God as they journeyed toward the center, where they spent time in concentrated prayer. Then, they'd slowly work their way back to the outside, carrying with them a spirit of renewal and refreshment into their everyday life.

If we practice being as intentional about each winding step of our journey of motherhood as those early pilgrims did walking a labyrinth, we'll begin to realize that we're not going around in circles. Each day takes us and our children one step closer to maturity and to God.

In Jeremiah 29:11, we read, "'For I know the plans I have for you,' declares the LORD, 'plans to prosper you and not to harm you, plans to give you hope and a future.'" Right now, those plans may include doing mountains of laundry, staying up all night with a sick child, or running countless carpools. Though the future we're looking toward may have many twists and turns down our labyrinth-like path, it's still there. Through patience, perseverance, and God's strength, our eventual arrival is sure.

Dear Lord, whatever I face today, remind me that you're by my side. If my journey feels slow, rocky, or confusing, help me to not lose heart. Renew my strength and remind me of my purpose. Amen.

A TIP TO TRY: When life feels overwhelming, take a walk around the block to regain perspective. Bundle up the kids and take them along if need be. Look for signs of God's creativity in the world around you as you go. Just a few minutes outdoors is like a boost of natural caffeine!

# Undercover Mother

So, my dear brothers and sisters,
be strong and immovable. Always work
enthusiastically for the Lord, for you know that
nothing you do for the Lord is ever useless.

—1 Corinthians 15:58 nlt

Have you ever watched a hamster on a wheel running as fast as it can but never getting anywhere? Yup, there are days when motherhood can feel just like that. You clean the kitchen, but before you walk out of the room someone sets another dish in the sink. As you're folding laundry, more dirty clothes are being stuffed into the hamper. You fill the car with gas, only to realize that you filled up the day before yesterday, and you haven't even driven out of town. To top it off, your own family may not seem to notice how much you do for them day in and day out. You not only feel like a hamster, you feel like an invisible, unappreciated one.

Working as hard as you can, while feeling as though you're being taken for granted, is never comfortable. It's an annoying little jab right in your pride. It taunts you, tempting you to slow down, cut a few corners, and do less than your best. After all, who's going to notice? You will.

The less effort we put into a job, the more we minimize the importance of that job in our own minds. And yes, God is watching, but not like a micromanaging boss who's ready to fire us at any moment. Rather, he's more like a cheerleader, encouraging us to love each other well and live up to whom he created us to be.

All of those little things we do for our family—cooking, cleaning, grocery shopping, changing diapers, running carpools—matter. They matter because the people we're serving by doing those things matter. The work we do as mothers isn't mindless busywork; it's love in action—love for our family and for the Lord who's entrusted them into our care.

Dear Lord, help me remember why I'm doing what I'm doing. Remind me that the chores I do are just another way of saying I love you to my family. Thank you for each one of them. Amen.

A TIP TO TRY: Your children crawl up into your lap when they need a hug. Remember that you can ask for snuggle time too. Although God is always near, sometimes we need real arms to hold us close. Little arms can hold great comfort.

# We All Need a Hero

"The Lord will fight for you;
you need only to be still."

—Exodus 14:14

The story is played out on movie screens over and over again. The heroine is in peril. It looks as though all is lost. Then, the hero swoops in to save the day. Even before the movie began, we knew everything was going to be okay in the end. Why do we never tire of the same storyline? It's because deep down we long for a hero to rescue us.

He already has. God humbled himself to take on human form and die on the cross for our sins. He came to earth solely to save us, but our hearts long for more. We want to know that those who love us here on earth would be heroes on our behalf. In other words, if our house was on fire, we trust they'd rescue us before trying to save the artwork on the walls. Our children long for this same kind of reassurance from us.

Do our kids know we have their back? Can they trust us to fight for them, protect them, and come to their rescue? Do they know how much we value them and understand that value doesn't fluctuate according to how "good" or "bad" they happen to be today?

Little things we do and say can undermine how we communicate love to our children. When we're tired, stressed, busy, or angry, we can unintentionally treat our children as interruptions or impositions. Our tone of voice, lack of eye contact, and dismissive attitude can leave them feeling confused, insecure, and isolated.

When we're at our weakest, it's easy to become self-focused and self-protective, but with God's help, we can reach out, instead of pulling in. We can better care for our children as we allow God to care for us.

Dear Lord, please prevent my own emotional needs from blinding me to the needs of my children. Help me find the words and actions I need to reassure them of my love and yours. Amen.

A TIP TO TRY: Large baby bibs make excellent super hero capes for playtime. Then when your little hero needs a snack, simply turn the bib around to the front. (Warning: Anytime children have something around their neck, such as a bib, cape, scarf, or dress-up jewelry, carefully supervise their play so what they're wearing doesn't accidentally get caught on something.)

# Refresh and Renew

Finally, my friends, keep your minds on
whatever is true, pure, right, holy, friendly,
and proper. Don't ever stop thinking about
what is truly worthwhile and worthy of praise.

—PHILIPPIANS 4:8 CEV

The demands of motherhood can be mind-numbing at
times: reading the same book aloud at bedtime for
the thirtieth day in a row; tending to one sick child after
another as the flu makes the rounds through your home;
helping your children practice spelling words, times
tables, or scales on the piano day after day after day.

When you've sung so many rounds of "Old MacDon-
ald" that even Noah couldn't possibly come up with
another animal sound to imitate, it's time to reboot your
brain. After all, when your phone, computer, or modem

starts acting a little funny, what's the first thing you try? Shut everything down and start it up again. We may not understand why this works, but all that matters is that it does.

God created our brains with much more intricacy and capacity than a computer, but like a computer, there are times when our brains seem to run a bit glitchy. Either we feel foggy-headed from monotony, or we can't turn our brain off at night because we're overly anxious or stressed. Both leave us feeling as though we're operating at less than our mental best.

God has built an automatic reboot function into our brains called a good night's sleep, but sometimes, that proves elusive or inadequate. His secondary back-up system can be found in Philippians 4:8. Taking a few minutes—as many times a day as needed—to meditate on God's Word, on his character, or simply on all of the blessings he's brought into your life can help clear your head, as well as encourage your heart. It's like a fresh start—anytime, anywhere.

Dear Lord, when I can't think straight my whole day feels off. Please help me get a good night's sleep, as well as remember to take breaks throughout the day to help realign my mind with yours. Amen.

A TIP TO TRY: If you like to check in on your sleeping children before you head to bed, place a thick rubber band over the doorknob in their room. Twist it so it makes an X and loop the other end of the band over the outside doorknob. Make sure the X in the center holds the depressed door latch in place. Then, you can open and close the door without making a sound that might wake a sleeping child.

# 44 Love Conquers All

The same way a loving father feels
toward his children—that's but a sample
of your tender feelings toward us,
your beloved children, who live in awe of you!

—PSALM 103:13 TPT

Love isn't always puppies and rainbows; sometimes, it's tarantulas and funnel clouds. It may be tough for a first-time mom to imagine her bundle of joy stirring up a barrel of trouble someday, but kids can be incredibly stubborn and self-centered—as can their parents.

However, parental love is an especially powerful bond. It isn't as fickle as romantic love. We don't fall in love with our children because they are good looking, are marvelous conversationalists, or have a quick wit; we love them sight unseen. It's the most unconditional love we can give, which means it's one of the best glimpses we have into how God feels about his own children, including us.

Romans 5:8 (GW) tells us, "Christ died for us while we were still sinners. This demonstrates God's love for us." As far as is humanly possible, this is the kind of love we want to have for our own children—unconditional, sacrificial, merciful, and kind. When our children are disobedient, unreasonable, or lash out in anger, let's keep in mind how frequently we treat our own heavenly Father the same way. Our children's hearts are not that different from our own. Therefore, learning to love them well means learning to temper our own internal storms. This includes apologizing when appropriate, both to them and to God.

It's easy to say, "Love conquers all," but a conquest implies a battle was fought somewhere along the way. Battles are never pretty, but that doesn't mean things have to get ugly. Anger, disagreements, and disappointment are inevitable when imperfect people enter into a relationship with one another, but as we work through our difficulties making our way toward reconciliation and forgiveness, love shows just how strong, beautiful, and resilient it really is.

Dear Lord, you know what stirs up anger most easily in me. Teach me to respond with love and reason when my kids push my emotional buttons. Make my love more like yours. Amen.

A TIP TO TRY: When anger, frustration, or disappointment leads a child to lash out with the words, "I hate you!" respond in a way that reflects God's own gracious love. Say, "I'm sorry you feel that way right now, but that's okay, because I love you enough for both of us."

# 45

# One of a Kind

> You made all the delicate, inner parts of my body
> and knit them together in my mother's womb.
> Thank you for making me so wonderfully complex!
> It is amazing to think about. Your workmanship
> is marvelous—and how well I know it.
>
> —Psalm 139:13–14 TLB

Becoming a mother is more than a privilege; it's an invitation to worship. From the moment we discover a new life growing inside us, we can't help but be awestruck by the wonder of it all. Another heart beating along with our own; receiving a swift kick from the inside; the moment we get to hold in our arms the miracle that's been growing in our womb; first steps; first words; and even watching our child sleep. There are so many moments that feel surprisingly sacred, even though we know the same scenario has been lived out in families all over the world since the dawn of time.

Yes, motherhood offers a unique call to worship, but let's remember who we're called to worship: the Creator, not his creation. No matter how obvious this may seem, our heart can be pulled in the opposite direction. Instead of raising our children, we can slide into a habit of living vicariously through them. Their successes and failures become our own. We pressure them to excel in music, because our parents couldn't afford piano lessons for us. We push them to attend our alma mater to extend our own legacy on campus. We strive to create pint-sized versions of ourselves who will "get it right" this time around.

Psalm 139 reminds us that God created each of us in a uniquely wonderful way. Even if our children choose to follow in our footsteps in certain areas, the path they take to get there needs to be their own. Let's reserve our worship for the one who truly knows us inside and out, our Creator, Father, Lord, and King.

Dear Lord, when I look at my children, may my profound love for them lead me back to worship you. I'm so grateful that you chose me to care for them. Amen.

A TIP TO TRY: Every face is unique—even at the dinner table. When you serve your kids dinner, make a face on their plate out of the food you've prepared. Kids will more readily eat snow pea eyebrows and a cherry tomato mouth than a spoonful of random veggies scooped onto their plate. If they're still hungry, allow them to fashion their own unique face out of the second servings they receive.

46

Family
Fanfare

"It is right to celebrate."
—LUKE 15:32 TLB

There's one phrase kids never seem to get tired of using. Whether they're riding a bike, jumping off a diving board, playing dress-up in a pair of our heels, or enjoying countless other scenarios where we happen to be within shouting range, there's nothing quite as unabashedly gleeful as a child shouting, "Mom, look at me! Look at me!"

We all crave an audience. Why else would we care if our post on social media receives so many "likes"? But the audience our kids crave most when they're young is us. Our approval, recognition, and pride in their accomplishments is paramount. While impromptu applause or a heartfelt, "Good for you!" is certainly appropriate, it's nice to go above and beyond in our admiration once in a while.

Why should birthdays and holidays have a monopoly on celebration? Good days, bad days, even ordinary run-of-the-mill days contain plenty of reasons to celebrate each member of our family. We don't need to go to a lot of trouble and expense. We can tie a balloon on a child's chair; stick a candle in the middle of tonight's lasagna; throw confetti; hang a "Hurray for YOU!" poster on the front door; or put a gold star on a child's forehead. No matter how you celebrate, the goal is to shine a spotlight on anyone who could use a little encouragement or recognition.

While we're at it, let's not forget to celebrate God. He never demands our attention or shouts, "Look at me!" By tying a balloon to an empty chair or asking each person around the table to share one thing they appreciate about God, we can celebrate Thanksgiving any day of the year.

Dear Lord, thanks to you, I have so much to celebrate. Show me how to make our family times more festive and fun. Amen.

A TIP TO TRY: If your celebration menu happens to include hot dogs, put the condiments and toppings in the bun before you put in the hot dog. This one simple step can reduce the amount of cleaning up you'll have to do afterward.

# Walk This Way

47

> The lovers of God will walk in integrity,
> and their children are fortunate to have
> godly parents as their examples.
>
> —Proverbs 20:7 tpt

How would you feel if your children lied to you, if they took money out of your purse without asking, or if a speeding ticket arrived in the mail with your child's name on it? Would you be angry? Shocked? Disappointed? Would a lecture on the importance of integrity be certain to follow?

Suppose the tables were turned. An acquaintance who's incredibly annoying invites you out, but you decline her invitation, saying you're too busy when you're not. You notice the server undercharged you for your entree at a nice restaurant, but you keep quiet, secretly glad you saved an extra five bucks. Or while driving fifteen miles over the speed limit, you notice a police car partially hidden behind a tree up ahead, so you slow down as you pass but speed right up again once you're out of sight.

Integrity isn't measured on a sliding scale; we either have it or we don't. That's not to say we're immune from making poor choices now and then, but when that happens, confession and repentance put us back on the right track. However, if we're always walking just a bit in the gray, prone to white lies and exaggeration, underreporting our income on our taxes just a smidge, or only speeding when there isn't a police car in sight, we're teaching our children that it's okay to cheat just a bit—as long as you don't get caught.

The next time our children are less than honest with us, let's be honest with ourselves. Let's take a close look at the example we're providing them, and let's be an example worth following.

Dear Lord, I want to be a woman of integrity, but I know there are areas in my life where I'm not totally honest, especially areas others can't see. Please forgive me. Give me the strength to do what's right. Amen.

A TIP TO TRY: **If you want your kids to follow in your footsteps, it's handy if they have their shoes on the right feet! Help little ones out by cutting a sturdy sticker in half. Put the left half of the sticker inside their left shoe and the other half inside the right. Show them how to match up the picture and then put the correct shoes on the corresponding feet.**

# 48

# Repeat Performance

And now a word to you parents.
Don't keep on scolding and nagging your children,
making them angry and resentful. Rather,
bring them up with the loving discipline the Lord
himself approves, with suggestions and godly advice.

—EPHESIANS 6:4 TLB

Think back. Way back, before digital downloads, CD players, cassette decks, and even eight-track tapes. Once upon a time there was a thing called a record. (If you're too young to have actually owned one, ask your parents to tell you all about them!) A record worked well as long as you treated it gently, but get one little scratch on the surface and your favorite song was reduced to repeating the same phrase over and over again … just like a mom when her kids won't do what they're told.

Nagging our kids can be as annoying as a broken record, and as a method of instruction or discipline, it isn't all that effective. If our kids ignore what we ask the first, second, and third time around, what will make the fourth time any different? Sure, our voice may get louder, our tone may get harsher, and we may add an "or else" at the end, but the result is usually the same. By the time the kids do what we've asked, everyone is frustrated, annoyed, and snarky with one another.

Let's stop the snark before it starts. Ask your children once to do something. Speak to them face-to-face, making eye contact, not yelling orders from somewhere down the hall. Then, give your kids a chance to respond. If they don't, ask a second time, adding a reasonable consequence to your request. If they still don't respond, don't ask a third time. Act on what you said you'd do.

Nagging is easy. Remaining even-tempered and consistent in discipline is not, but it's worth it. Whatever we're asking our children to do is never as important as who we're helping our children grow up to become.

Dear Lord, help me discern between disobedience, distraction, and absentmindedness in my children. Give me the wisdom to know how love and discipline can work together in a positive way. Amen.

A TIP TO TRY: Use music to help kids clean their room in "record" time. Choose a song they enjoy. Challenge them to finish cleaning their room before the song ends. Set standards of what needs to be done and shoving everything in the closet doesn't count. Turn on the music and let the cleaning begin!

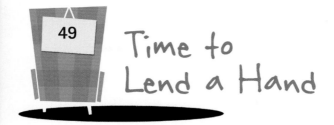

49

# Time to Lend a Hand

Whoever refreshes others
will be refreshed.

—Proverbs 11:25

Busy moms need a break. So do busy families. For a week or so every year, that break extends beyond a night out or a weekend away into full-fledged vacation mode. It doesn't matter whether we travel halfway around the world or plan a stay-cation in our own backyard, family vacations give us the opportunity to step out of our daily routine long enough to discover something new about the world, ourselves, and those we love.

There's nothing wrong with planning a vacation that focuses on family fun and relaxation. But there's another option that can draw families closer together, as well as awaken a sense of compassion and gratitude in our hearts;

it's a vacation where we expand our knowledge of the world around us and the people who share it with us.

Life is too short and the world is too big to explore everything God's created, but with a bit of planning, curiosity, and spunk, we can actually make a positive difference in the world. We can also help our children better understand the incredible diversity that exists outside the confines of our own home, culture, traditions, race, and socio-economic level.

By spending at least one day of our free time serving those in need, our entire family will become more aware of the privileges we enjoy, especially those we take for granted. We can serve meals to the homeless, read to the elderly, help stock a food pantry, join a church mission trip, or visit a school or orphanage abroad. The list and needs go on and on.

Serving others isn't a chore; it's a door inviting us to reach out and touch a life that could have been ours. Once that door is open, there's more room for gratitude and compassion to grow.

Dear Lord, over and over again in your Word, you talk about your love for widows, orphans, and the poor. Help your compassion for "the least of these" take root in me and my family. Amen.

A TIP TO TRY: Jesus said, "The poor will always be with you" (John 12:8 ICB). This includes vacation time. When making vacation plans, contact a humanitarian agency or local church based near your destination. Find out how your family can lend a hand while you're in town. Use your experience to start a discussion with your kids about how your lives differ from the lives of those you served.

# 50

# All in Good Time

In the morning, O LORD, hear my voice.
In the morning I lay my needs in front of you,
and I wait.

—PSALM 5:3 GW

When a newborn's hunger kicks in, it's no use trying to explain that Mom can't possibly breastfeed right now because she's stuck behind the wheel in a traffic jam. The infant will continue crying until his need for nourishment is met. We don't get upset when our baby responds this way. After all, wailing is a perfectly acceptable, age-appropriate response.

However, when our toddler or teenager throws a fit because they want this or that and they want it *now*, we're far less empathetic. Instead of chastising them, perhaps we should be more open with them about how there are times when we feel that very same way; such as, when we call customer service and are repeatedly put on hold, when the Internet is moving at a glacial pace, or when we have to postpone our vacation because our savings went to pay for unexpected car repairs.

In a world where same-day delivery, living on credit, and having sex before marriage are considered the norm, the concept of delayed gratification seems almost archaic. If we want something badly enough, chances are there's a way to get it. Fast.

Unfortunately, being able to fill our wants and needs in record time can adversely affect our ability to wait and waiting has so many wonderful lessons to teach us: it provides us with time to change our minds; it saves us from making emotionally driven decisions; it allows longing, anticipation, and appreciation to grow in ways that instant gratification never could; and it helps us learn to accept that God's timing isn't always in line with our own.

Waiting isn't easy, but it holds so many benefits for us and our children. The more we view it as a teacher instead of a bother, the less frustrated we'll be.

Dear Lord, I know your timing is always best, but that doesn't mean I always wait for your guidance before pushing my own agenda forward. Teach me what it means to wait on you. Amen.

A TIP TO TRY: Plant an herb garden in your kitchen window to help your children better understand the benefits of waiting. Together, check on its growth every day. Once it matures, help your children pick the herbs and use them to season family meals.

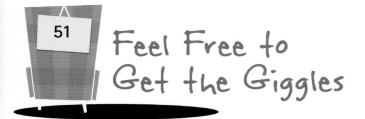

# 51

# Feel Free to Get the Giggles

How we laughed and sang for joy.
And the other nations said,
"What amazing things the Lord has done for them."
—Psalm 126:2 TLB

Kids are natural gigglers. They can find humor in any situation, including those times when we wish they didn't. But as we age, our guffaws usually grow quieter. We become more reserved. Life doesn't seem quite as funny anymore. There's more than enough tragedy and heartache in the world to temper our ruckus laughter into a wistful smile. But this is one area where our children can teach Mom a thing or two, and luckily for us, laughter is extremely contagious.

God's the one who originally gave us the gift of laughter. He wove it into our DNA. This gift isn't reserved for special occasions, like the good china. Keeping a child-like sense of humor close at hand at all times can help us maintain a more positive perspective on life. It also enables us to laugh more easily at ourselves, which helps keep us humble.

Interestingly enough, a common stereotype of a woman who chooses to live a life that pleases God is of a dour, joyless, tight-lipped matron. Perhaps it's time to risk showing the world a more accurate picture. Proverbs 31:25 describes a godly woman as "clothed with strength and dignity; she can laugh at the days to come." When we're secure in our faith, and the faithfulness of our God, we can relax enough to laugh at the future. We can be loyal, as well as light-hearted, godly, and still prone to giggle.

Encouraging laughter in our home adds a certain ease to family life. Let's make it our business to know what tickles our children's funny bone, as well as our own. Then, let the giggles begin.

Dear Lord, please help our home be a place of love and laughter. Show me what I can do to nurture both in a way that pleases you. Amen.

A TIP TO TRY: Be intentional about encouraging laughter in your home. Share a joke every evening at the dinner table. Watch humorous movies together. Reminisce over funny family faux pas. Wrestle on the floor and play "tickle monster." Whether in public or private, do what you can to make laughter a happy, healthy family habit.

# 52 Our Bittersweet Blessing

When Christ comes again,
I can be happy because my work was not wasted.
I ran in the race and won.

—PHILIPPIANS 2:16 ICB

It's a mother's job to teach her children how to live without her—and one of the toughest parts of the job is being successful! Depending on the age of our children, the empty nest may feel like it's a lifetime away or right around the corner. Regardless of how we feel, that day will eventually come. When it does, the house will be cleaner, quieter, and we can transform that empty bedroom into a craft nook and listen to "our" music in the car. But like every changing season of life, there will be things we look forward to and others we'll be sad to leave behind.

For instance, when our kids are young, our purpose as a mom is fairly clear. We change our children's diapers, feed them, bathe them, drive the carpool; everything they can't do themselves. So, we potty train them, teach them how to maneuver a spoon, bathe themselves, and later on, how to drive a car. We do our very best to work ourselves out of a job. But then what?

As our children mature, so should we. Even during the busiest seasons of motherhood, we need to afford ourselves room to grow, to learn something new, to challenge ourselves, to reach out beyond our family circle, and to thoughtfully consider what our next step will be after our children have left the nest.

Being a mom is a role filled with purpose and blessing, but it's only one of the roles God created us to fill. We have so much more to give and receive. Let's grab hold of the joys of today with one hand, while extending the other toward the possibilities of tomorrow. We're still in this race of living and loving until God takes us home.

Dear Lord, thank you for the privilege of being a mom. Please challenge me to continue to grow right along with my kids. Help me anticipate every new season with a sense of joy and adventure. Amen.

A TIP TO TRY: Schedule time alone with God. Have a notebook or journal and your Bible on hand. Ask God to help you see who you are apart from being a mom and to contemplate the next season of your life, whether that season is one where your kids start school or are leaving the nest. Pray, journal, draw, dream ... and remember to give thanks for it all.